Strange & Divine

JAMES S. DORCELY

Printed in the United States of America.

For more information, or to book an event, contact

Website: www.jamessdorcely.com
Email: info@jamessdorcely.com

Edited by Linda Chrissie Gray
Cover design by Izabela Ciesinska
Interior Design by Carlo

CONTENTS

FOREWORD
NATHAN S. FRENCH, PH.D.

One distinctive of biblical study that I have tried to instill into my students—fixed within my own mind by my teachers—is that serious readers of the word of God ought not to be afraid of the editors of scripture. Within our circles of Christianity, we have no issue imagining the authors of scripture and their importance, but rarely do we give credit to those who edited the text which we have faithfully received in its present form. Generally, for advanced students of Hebrew, such a claim is easily recognized, as it does not take long to notice various editorial seams throughout the Hebrew grammar of scripture, seams which occur in many books, narratives, and poetic lines of the Hebrew Bible. To take it a step further, we never stop to reflect on the divine inspiration of these texts while placing the authorial intent of scripture side by side with the editorial intent of scripture, both of which have the Divine Author and Editor as its source.

In his book, Strange & Divine, James S. Dorcely applies this aspect of God's editorial activity to our own lives by following the editorial work of the Spirit in the life of one of the most important and primal women in all of scripture, namely, the Egyptian slave, Hagar. Though short in written material, the episodic nature of her story—one filled with assurance, jubilation, and prominence, followed by the exactitude of oppressive norms, emotional turmoil, pain, and the threat of the never-ending truth that sin and death are always near in the experience of her and her young child's exile into the wilderness—carries within it the themes so readily apparent in the circumstances of humanity, both ancient and modern. Though the great patriarch and matriarch of ancient Israel are the cause of her exile, their descendants, too, will experience much the same throughout the remainder of the Hebrew Scriptures, themes of exilic wilderness wandering that occur again and again and again.

It is here, on this thematic chord of separation, that James S. Dorcely focuses in on the strange and divine editorial seams that guide the reader to weave their own lives around threads within the story of Hagar that though begin in great despair ultimately end up with divine promises of forgiveness, care, restoration, presence, and hope. Written with erudition toward what scholarship provides for interpretation on the one hand, but focused toward the practical for reflection, devotion, and prayer on the other, James S. Dorcely has provided an exceptional read with sensitive attention to the Hebrew of the text and to the literary features that bring out meaning for us all; meaning derived from the experience of a mother with her young son and their awareness together that there is a God who never leaves nor forsakes, but who is always there, in their pain and in ours, in their suffering and in ours, and in their exile and in ours.

Nathan S. French

Nathan S. French, Ph.D.
Associate Professor of Hebrew Bible and the Ancient Near East
Graduate School of the College of Theology & Ministry
Oral Roberts University

DEDICATION

To my biological mother, Claire-Melie Dorcely, who trained me in the way of the Lord.

To my adoptive mother, Fredeline Dorcely, whose love and sacrifice have made my success possible.

To my spiritual fathers Pastor Pierre E. Charles, Evangelist Stevenson Calixte and Pastor Vitalhern Marcelin, thank you for your lasting impact on my life and walk with God.

To Wilson Dorcely, who kept asking for the book long before it was finished, thank you for believing in it before it existed.

To the Dorcely family, siblings, cousins, and encouragers, your presence gave me roots and strength.

To my ministry companion, Dwoodmyr Dorcely, thank you for walking closely with me in faith, vision, and purpose.

To my cousin and friend, Cedeline Dorcely and Wilder Dorcely, thank you for your steady support and care.

To my dear friends, Davins Manasse, Cliff Florestal, and Berlyne Florestal, your encouragement and presence have been a gift along the way.

And to my beloved God-daughters, Joi Ava Dorcely and Raelynn A. Etienne, may your stories be written by the hand of the God who sees, loves, and redeems.

ACKNOWLEDGMENTS

I am deeply grateful to Dr. French, whose wisdom and mentorship guided me through the theological heart of this book. From the earliest drafts to final reflections, your encouragement helped me remain faithful to both Scripture and the God behind it.

I am sincerely thankful to Dr. Easterling, who carefully read Chapters 1 and 2 and personally reached out with thoughtful feedback. Your sociological insight deepened the clarity and impact of those chapters, reminding me that theology and sociology can, and should, coexist.

Thank you to Dr. Bill Buker, whose attentive reading of the first chapter shaped the foundation of this book and clarified how readers are invited into the story.

To Dr. Kirk, thank you for taking the time to read and encourage me throughout this process. Your support gave me confidence to keep moving forward.

I am also grateful to Mayah Welsh, whose artistic gift brought this project to life through her beautiful illustration, capturing the heart of this story in image as well as words.

And finally, to Martine Dorcely and Rasheeda Burgess, thank you for reading this manuscript with curiosity and care. Your support meant a great deal along the way.

INTRODUCTION

Have you ever felt caught in someone else's story? Have you ever felt like your life is a patchwork of choices made by others, like people have written their own lines into your story without your permission? Maybe it was the situation into which you were born. Maybe it was abuse, mistreatment, or neglect you've experienced, you name it. Sometimes these things shape the story of our lives more than we'd like to admit. At the end of the day, it can feel like much of what has happened to you is the result of others' decisions. And when you've finally had the chance to make choices for yourself, they may have been shaped by pressure or frustration, leading to decisions that hurt more than they healed.

Yes, we believe that God knows and writes our stories before we are born (Psalm 139:16). But what happens when the way your life unfolds doesn't look anything like what God would have written? What happens when pain, sickness, rejection, or humiliation take over the pages? Surely that wasn't in the book God wrote for your life, was it? You're right to wonder. Many parts of our lives fall out of alignment with what God had in mind. So, what does God do with the parts that were never meant to be there? The brokenness, the violations, the pages you wish you could tear out? That is exactly what this book endeavors to answer.

Strange and Divine is written on the unwavering truth that God is not only the Author of your life, but also the Editor of your story. Through these pages, you'll be invited to explore how

God intervenes in human narratives, not by erasing the past, but by redeeming it. This truth comes alive in the story of Hagar, an Egyptian slave girl caught in someone else's story.

HAGAR'S STORY

Hagar is one of the earliest women to appear in Scripture, alongside Sarah, Rebekah, Rachel, and Leah. Yet the pages devoted to her in the Hebrew Bible are few, just two chapters (Genesis 16 and 21), with a brief mention in the genealogy section in Genesis 25. Hagar's life was marked by betrayal, mistreatment, and misunderstanding at the hands of Sarah, her mistress, Abraham's wife. And yet, within her story, God reveals a powerful truth: in His just and compassionate nature, He always sides with the oppressed.

Compelled into a union with Abraham, an older man she did not choose, Hagar became the second wife of the Hebrew patriarch. This was not a story of love or desire, but of exploitation: Sarah sought to use Hagar's youthful body to bear the child she herself could not have. In many ways, it was an ancient practice resembling surrogacy. But Hagar knew that the child she bore would never truly be considered hers. Out of that frustration, she began to wield the only power she thought she had, her pregnancy, as a weapon against her mistress. This, in turn, provoked Sarah to retaliate with harsher treatment, resulting in Hagar's escape to the desert. All of this unfolds in the opening of Genesis 16. During that time, God remained silent, though not absent, and certainly not indifferent.

Yet even in these painful circumstances, the hand of the Divine is unmistakable. Hagar became the first woman in Scripture to encounter God directly, receiving a promise for her son that echoed the covenant given to Abraham. Her story is one of paradox: suffering and deliverance, rejection and divine recognition, loneliness and presence, scarcity and abundance. It is precisely this mixture that makes Hagar's story both strange and divine.

As we trace how God rewrote her story, adding His own lines without deleting the pain, you'll find hope for your own. God still redeems what others have mishandled. And yes, He still edits the lines that were never meant to be part of your story.

Each chapter includes a central theme from Hagar's journey, along with four reflection questions and one prayer point. You're invited to pause, reflect, and even journal as you go, because this isn't just Hagar's story; It's yours too.

So, how does a woman like Hagar, unseen, unchosen, and unheard, become part of a divine story? To answer that, we begin with Abraham and Sarah, two people with a promise, a problem, and a plan. And in the middle of it, they write Hagar into their story.

1

HOW HAGAR BECAME PART OF THE STORY

When God first called Abram, He made three significant promises: land, descendants, and a great name (Genesis 12:1–3, 7).[1] Abram believed God, took his wife, his nephew Lot, and all his possessions, left his country, his people, and his father's household, and followed God wholeheartedly to the land of Canaan. God's promise to Abram became the defining force in his walk with God. As the Prophet Habakkuk reminds us, two things are always true about God's promises: first, they will come to pass, and second, they will take time. They won't happen immediately (Habakkuk 2:3).

THE PROMISES OF GOD ALWAYS COME TO PASS

It is amazing that Abram believed God the moment He spoke to him. Really, Abram? Aren't you going to ask questions? No hesitation, no "But Lord, how will this work?" He simply believed! This kind of certainty in God's promises is a recurring theme throughout Scripture. The Old Testament prophets, too, understood that when God declares something or makes a promise, it is as good as done, even before it happens. The Hebrew language has a fascinating grammatical structure related to prophecy. In Biblical prophecy, there is a verb tense called the "prophetic perfect." This means that when a prophet speaks of a future event, he often writes it in the past tense. Why? Because Hebrew prophets understood that when God gives a prophecy or makes a promise, it never fails. To them, it is already accomplished, so they conjugate the verb in the past tense as a declaration of its certainty.

As for an example, the Prophet Isaiah prophesied about the suffering Messiah in Isaiah 53, saying, "He was bruised for our iniquities" (Isaiah 53:5). A careful reader will notice that Isaiah

---

[1] Unless otherwise indicated, Scripture quotations are taken from the *Holy Bible, New International Version*®, NIV®. Copyright ©1973, 1978, 1984, 2011 by Biblica, Inc.™ Used by permission. All rights reserved worldwide.

wrote these words centuries before Christ came. Yet, he spoke as though it had already happened. Why? Because, in the mind of a Hebrew prophet, when God makes a promise, it is as good as done. They understood that God's word is certain, and His promises are inevitable. This same understanding explains why Abram believed in God so much. He knew that if God had spoken, it would surely come to pass, no matter his present circumstances. In Paul's words, "For no matter how many promises God has made, they are "Yes" in Christ..." (2 Corinthians 1:20).

THE PROMISES OF GOD TAKE TIME

"Immediately," two obstacles stood between "the two main promises of land and descendants."[2] First, the Promised Land appeared infertile. The Bible mentions that there was a famine in Canaan, making it seem like an unsuitable place for God's blessing (Genesis 12:10). The cause of the land's infertility is not mentioned here. However, at that time, it was likely that the famine in Canaan was caused by a lack of rain, making it difficult for crops to grow[3]. Second, Sarai, Abram's wife, was infertile. The Bible introduces her as barren, unable to bear children (Genesis 11:30). This made God's promise of numerous descendants seem impossible.

It is tempting, and rightly so, to wonder whether both the famine in the land and the barrenness of Sarai's womb represent a reversal of God's creational blessing. In the beginning, God blessed the man and the woman, commanding them to be fruitful and multiply (Genesis 1:28). The ground, too, was blessed before The Fall, untouched by curse. But here, we are confronted with the opposite of what ought to be: a barren womb and an unfruit-

---

[2] Allen P. Ross, *Genesis*, in *Cornerstone Biblical Commentary: Genesis, Exodus*, ed. Philip W. Comfort, vol. 1 (Carol Stream, IL: Tyndale House, 2008), 115.

[3] Stephen J. Binz, *Abram: Father of All Believers* (Collegeville, MN: Liturgical Press, 2011), 19.

ful land. This disruption suggests that God's promise to Abram was more than a personal blessing, it was a kind of re-creation.[4]

WHEN FAITH TAKES DETOUR

The famine forced Abram to leave the land of Canaan, so he went to stay in Egypt for a while. The story does not mention Abram consulting the God of the promise before making this decision. This is not an example of Abram putting his faith in action; instead, it is Abram putting his faith in *his own* action. Human effort, even at its best, still falls short of God's plan.

To prevent himself from being killed in Egypt due to his wife's praiseworthy beauty, Abram said to Sarai, "Say you are my sister, so that I will be treated well and my life will be spared because of you" (Genesis 12:13). Some ancient Egyptian writings suggest that it was not uncommon for the Pharaoh to take foreigners' wives and kill their husbands if they stood in the way.[5] This historical context clarifies why this is the first instance of a patriarch lying about his marital status to protect himself, but not the only occurrence. The author of Genesis recounts two more such incidents: In Genesis 20:1-8, Abram lies to King Abimelech, and in Genesis 26:1-6, Isaac and Rebekah deceive Abimelech in a similar manner.

It must be noted that the issue here is not merely that Abram lied, if lying is even a concern, it would be a half-truth because Sarai was indeed his half-sister. This is confirmed in Genesis 20:12, where Abram states, "She really is my sister, the daughter of my father though not of my mother; and she became my wife." The greater problem is that by giving Sarai to Pharaoh,

---

[4] Through Abram, and ultimately through **Jesus** (Galatians 3:16), all families of the earth would be blessed, and those who belong to Christ are heirs of that promise by faith (Galatians 3:29).

[5] Nahum M. Sarna, *The JPS Torah Commentary: Genesis* (Philadelphia: Jewish Publication Society, 1989), 95.

Abram jeopardized God's plan, as Sarai was central to the promise of a great nation. Some have noted, "The man whom God has promised children now has no wife with whom to create them."[6]

GETTING CAUGHT IN SOMEONE'S ELSE STORY

In His faithfulness, God remembered His promise to Abram and intervened to prevent Pharaoh from taking Sarai as his wife, and the Lord dealt harshly with Pharaoh, afflicting his household with plagues (Genesis 12:17). Terrified by the judgment he and his house had suffered, Pharaoh quickly returned Sarai to Abram and ordered them to leave Egypt. Not only did Pharaoh release Sarai, but he also allowed Abram to leave with all the wealth he had accumulated in Egypt, including sheep, cattle, male and female donkeys, and male and female servants (Genesis 12:16, 20). Among those female servants was a young Egyptian girl named Hagar (Genesis 16:1).

It seems that the famine in the land was no longer a concern for the patriarch. While the Bible does not suggest that Canaan had suddenly become a land "flowing with milk and honey," Abram was now wealthy enough that the infertility of the land no longer affected him. The promise of land seemed more reasonable now that he had the resources to sustain himself. However, one major obstacle remained; Sarai was still barren. Unlike before, when they sought a solution by going to Egypt, this time, Egypt came to them. Hagar's entrance into the story compels the reader to question her role: Is she a slave, a solution, or part of a divine set-up?

---

[6] A. Carter Shelley, *Preaching — Genesis 12–36* (St. Louis, MO: Chalice Press, 2001).

WRITE
YOUR STORY

1. Describe a time when you found yourself caught in a story you didn't choose.

2. **What does Abram and Sarai's decision to take matters into their own hands reveal about their faith, and how does that decision lead to Hagar's entrance into the story?**

3. In your own life, how can you discern the difference between faithfully acting on God's promises and relying on your own plans to fulfill them?

4. When you realize you've acted in your own strength instead of following God's leading, how would you pray for His mercy and redirection? Remember how God intervened for Abram so that he would not lose Sarai, ask Him to show you the same kind of mercy when you miss the mark.

WRITE YOUR PRAYER

Take a moment to speak to God about what you've just read and written. What do you need to say to Him? What do you want to ask or surrender? Use the space below to write your own prayer, from your heart to His.

2

IS HAGAR A SLAVE, A SOLUTION, OR PART OF A DIVINE SET-UP?

The story of Hagar in Genesis 16 introduces what may be considered the first instance of surrogacy in the Bible. Unlike modern surrogacy, where a woman agrees and consents to bear a child for another through medical procedures, this arrangement is marked by social pressure, silence, and the absence of true consent. The first part of verse 1 highlights the second major obstacle to God's promise to Abram: Sarai's inability to bear children. Although their childlessness was first mentioned in Genesis 11:30, no explanation was given at that time, not even their old age. But here, Sarai offers her own interpretation, declaring, "The Lord has kept me from having children" (Genesis 16:2). Her explanation reflects the ancient belief that "barrenness and fertility was ascribed to God."[7]

The second part of the verse mentions Hagar's first appearance in the Biblical narrative (Genesis 16:1), where the narrator provides her full background, her origin, social status and name: "An Egyptian slave named Hagar." Two women are mentioned in the first verse, yet they stand in stark contrast to one another. As Phyllis Trible rightly observes in *Texts of Terror*, "Sarai the Hebrew is married, rich, and free; she is also old and barren. Hagar the Egyptian is single, poor, and bonded; she is also young and fertile."[8]

It is important to recognize the immense pressure Sarai faced due to her childlessness. In the Ancient Near East, infertility was not only a source of shame but also carried legal and social expectations. Mesopotamian marriage contracts stipulated that "the infertile wife was required to search for a surrogate mother"[9] so that the husband might have descendants. Like her husband,

---

[7] David J. Zucker and Moshe Reiss, *The Matriarchs of Genesis: Seven Women, Five Views* (Eugene, OR: Wipf & Stock, 2015), 54; Kindle ed., 89.

[8] Phyllis Trible, *Texts of Terror: Literary-Feminist Readings of Biblical Narratives*, 40th Anniversary Edition (Minneapolis: Fortress Press, 2022), 10.

[9] John E. Hartley, *Genesis*, vol. 1 of *New International Biblical Commentary* (Peabody, MA: Hendrickson Publishers, 2000), 164.

who once felt responsible for providing for his family and therefore left the Promised Land, Canaan, to sojourn in Egypt, Sarai also felt responsible for providing a child to her husband, whether the Lord was involved or not. So far, it seems like her best, if not her only, option is her servant Hagar. She urged Abram, "Go, sleep with my slave; perhaps I can build a family through her" (Genesis 16:2).

Now, Hagar is no longer just a servant. She is a potential surrogate mother, a solution or a means to an end in Sarai's desperate attempt to secure the promise child. But is that all she is? Given the setting, this chapter invites us to reflect on an intriguing question: Is Hagar a slave, a solution, or part of a divine set-up?

If we answer this question through the lens of the couple, the response will be straightforward, but flawed. Sarai and Abram define Hagar solely by her function, not her personhood. Yet, up to this point (Genesis 16:1–6), the passage does not explicitly describe Hagar's feelings about her situation, nor does the narrator give her a voice "in this drama,"[10] leaving us to wonder: What is Hagar feeling, caught in the middle of someone else's plan? How does she make sense of herself as her body is used, her voice ignored, and her name erased from the mouths of those in power? At this point in the story, Cooley's *Looking-Glass Self* comes alive. This is a sociological theory that explains how we come to know ourselves through the mirror of other people's eyes. In simple terms, it means that the way others see us, and how we imagine they see us, can either build or break our sense of worth.

The Mirror of Identity

Charles Cooley's *Looking-Glass Self* theory suggests that we form our identity based on how we believe others perceive us. According to the American sociologist, we are not merely what we think

---

[10] Zucker and Reiss, *The Matriarchs of Genesis*, Kindle ed., 89.

we are, but what we believe others think we are.[11] This concept plays out in everyday life; one does not need to be a sociologist to grasp its truth. For example, a recent viral video on Instagram shows a child leaving the soccer field and running excitedly to their mother, saying, "Mommy, I'm part of the team! I'm having so much fun!" The comment section is filled with gratitude and joy, as viewers celebrate the heartwarming moment of a child experiencing a sense of belonging.

From the child's perspective, they must be a good team player, regardless of their actual soccer skills. In their mind, they are just as great as Lionel Messi or Cristiano Ronaldo. This belief doesn't necessarily depend on their actual abilities, but on the coach's recognition. Because the coach allowed them to join the team, the child assumes that the coach sees them as a skilled player, and, therefore, they see themselves that way too. This self-perception is shaped by three key elements: how they imagine the coach sees them, how they interpret that perception, and how they **feel** about themselves as a result. All of us have experienced this in some way. Think back to your own childhood: what words were said, or left unsaid, that built or broke your self-esteem? Have parents, siblings, or friends ever acted in ways that made you feel valued, intelligent, or deeply loved? A simple phrase like "I love you" or "You're so smart" can anchor a positive self-image.

The opposite is also true. When we are mistreated or repeatedly hear negative words about our abilities or identity, we internalize those messages. In fact, much of what we think others believe about us may not be true. But it still shapes our self-perception. This is the heart of the *Looking-Glass Self.* We see ourselves the way we imagine others see us. And this theory provides a powerful lens for understanding how Hagar may have seen herself, filtered through how Abram and Sarai treated her.

---

[11] Charles Horton Cooley, *Human Nature and the Social Order* (New York: Scribner's, 1902), 152.

IS HAGAR A SLAVE?

Careful readers will notice that while the narrator introduces Hagar by name, and later, God calls her by name, both Abram and Sarai never do. They refer to her only by her social role: "the slave woman." For example, when Sarai, desperate for a child, urges Abram to use Hagar, she commands, "Go, sleep with my slave…" (Genesis 16:2). Later, when Sarai complains to Abram, he responds, "Your slave is in your hands…" (Genesis 16:6). Perhaps the most striking dismissal comes when Sarai demands Hagar's expulsion: "Get rid of that slave woman" (Genesis 21:10). It is reasonable to infer that Hagar began to see herself through the lens of her master and mistress, as a nameless servant whose worth was tied only to her function. By refusing to use her name, Abram and Sarai didn't just ignore her identity, they taught her to see herself as insignificant. Over time, she internalized their disregard, forming an identity shaped not by who she is, but by what she thinks she is to others.

When others strip us of dignity, ignore our names, or reduce us to roles, it can cloud our vision of ourselves. Even when we know, deep down, that we are more than what they see, their silence, or belittlement, speak louder than God's truth. Hagar is not an exception. Her story reminds us that unless someone calls us by our true name, we may begin to believe we are only what others think we are. At this point in the story, Hagar sees herself as nothing more than a slave. But before we can fully explore whether that is all she is, we must first ask: Is she merely a solution, or part of something divine?

IS HAGAR A SOLUTION?

Fortunately, there is more to Hagar than simply a slave girl. To Sarai, she is also a potential solution to the couple's problem. Therefore, "Sarai, [Abram's wife,] took her Egyptian slave Hagar and gave her to her husband to be his wife" (Genesis 16:3). The Hebrew word translated to as "wife" is *isha,* suggesting that she does not merely become a concubine (*pilegesh).*"[12] She, indeed, became Abram's second wife. It is tempting to note the irony in this situation: Sarai, the woman who was once given away to an Egyptian king by her husband, is now giving her husband away to an Egyptian slave. Sarai, who was once "the oppressed, becomes the oppressor."[13] According to the custom of the time, the act of giving one's slave to one's husband as wife for childbearing was not considered unethical.[14] In a sense, it was an early form of surrogacy, but a far more personal arrangement with far fewer boundaries, as it required the husband to sleep with the surrogate herself. While this is the first instance in Scripture where natural surrogacy appears, it is not the only one. A few chapters later, Rachel and Leah also offer their servants to Jacob as wives (Genesis 30:3–9).

Although Sarai's intention here was purely that "Hagar is to be her surrogate womb,"[15] "by giving Hagar to Abram as a wife, she has enhanced the status of the servant to become herself correspondingly lowered in the eyes of Hagar."[16] This shift reshaped Hagar's self-image. Therefore "When Abram slept with Hagar, and she conceived" (Genesis 16:3), she began to see herself differently. No longer was she just a nameless slave; she realizes that, unlike her mistress, she is young and fruitful. She knows that through her, the long-desperate couple can build a family and preserve the continuity of Abram's name. Hagar interprets this shift as confirmation that she is the solution to Sarai and Abram's

---

[12] Zucker and Reiss, *The Matriarchs of Genesis*, Kindle ed., 90.

[13] Phyllis Trible and Letty M. Russell, eds., *Hagar, Sarai, and Their Children: Jewish, Christian, and Muslim Perspectives* (Louisville, KY: Westminster John Knox Press, 2006), 38.

[14] Zucker and Reiss, *The Matriarchs of Genesis*, Kindle ed., 89.

[15] Zucker and Reiss, 89.

[16] Trible, *Texts of Terror*, 12.

problem. As John E. Hartley observes, her "new position and her pregnancy boosted her self-image,"[17] so much that "by her attitude and probably by her words, she began to make life miserable for Sarai."[18] Nevertheless, what confronts the reader here is to wonder whether Hagar is simply taking advantage of the moment to confront Sarai for how she has been treated all these years or whether something far deeper is going on.

FROM SLAVE TO WIFE, AND FROM WIFE TO SLAVE

It is not explicitly stated why Hagar, now the second wife of Abram, was not fully content with her new status and behaved well to remain in that position. After all, this was a dramatic shift, from being an Egyptian slave to becoming Abram's second wife and carrying what she believed to be the child of the promise.

Why did she feel the need to despise Sarai? Perhaps, since despite this elevation, she remained painfully aware that the son she carried would never truly be hers. She was merely an instrument, merely building someone else's house. She knew she would not have the joy of loving a child as her own, nor would she be loved unconditionally. She knew the day would come when the child would be born and taken from her.[19] It's important to remember that the child was never truly meant to be Hagar's. He would belong to Sarai. In that moment, she chose to hold on to her pride, believing she would not be able to hold on to the child she loved. She took refuge in the vanity of her thoughts and looked down

---

[17] Hartley, *Genesis*, Kindle ed., 228.

[18] *Genesis: The Old Testament, The Complete Biblical Library* (Springfield, MO: World Library Press, 1994), 131.

[19] Henry M. Morris, *The Genesis Record: A Scientific and Devotional Commentary on the Book of Beginnings* (Grand Rapids: Baker Book House, 1976), Kindle ed., 457.

upon her mistress, even though it would ultimately come at the cost of her demotion, humiliation, and mistreatments.

Sarai refused to be treated the way she treated others. When the consequences of her own choices turned against her, she quickly shifted the blame. She went to Abram and complained,

> You are responsible for the wrong I am suffering. I put my slave in your arms, and now that she knows she is pregnant, she despises me. May the LORD judge between you and me (Genesis 16:5).

Here the author further acknowledges Hagar's elevated position as a wife by recounting that Sarai had to complain to Abram or indirectly ask for permission before reacting to Hagar's insult. Abram, probably tired of being caught in the rivalry between his two wives, authorized his first wife to deal with Hagar as she pleased, which returned Hagar to her previous status as a slave.[20] Sarai's jealousy got the best of her, and she mistreated Hagar. The Hebrew term *innah*, translated as "mistreatment," is the same word used to describe the suffering the Israelites would endure in Egypt.[21] (Genesis 15:13; Exodus 1:12; cf. 2 Samuel 13, and Amnon's rape of Tamar). Perhaps, this deliberate choice of wording serves a dual purpose: first, as a foreshadowing that one day the Hebrews will suffer the same mistreatment in Egypt; and second, maybe the most probable, to emphasize the severity of Hagar's suffering, which likely included physical harm.[22]

Undoubtedly, Hagar's sense of superiority, based on her new status, was merely her own perception after all. Suddenly, the mere formal complaint of Sarai was enough to demote her from a wife to a slave. She then realized that to Abram, Sarai was the

---

[20] Hartley, *Genesis*, Kindle ed., 229.

[21] Hartley, 229.

[22] Zucker and Reiss, *The Matriarchs of Genesis*, Kindle ed., 92.

beloved wife, while she remained an instrument of convenience, despite her youthfulness and fertility. Hagar was surely disappointed.

This illustrates the danger of basing our self-worth and self-esteem solely on societal standards such as status, position, and opinion of others. Human validation is fleeting and unreliable. Instead, our self-image should be grounded in the unchanging truth that we are created in the image of God (Genesis 1:27) and we are "fearfully and wonderfully made" (Psalms 139:14). When we recognize that our identity is shaped by how God sees us, we are shielded from the disappointments of human validation. Hagar learned this the hard way. Betrayal, disappointment and mistreatment caused her to escape. Wounded and alone, she wandered into the wilderness, not knowing what would come next.

IS HAGAR PART OF A DIVINE SET-UP?

Imagine Hagar in the desert, standing before a series of mirrors, each one reflecting a version of her that was forced upon her (see figure). In one, she is Sarai's slave. In another, Abram's instrument, used for their desires, not known for her humanity. Each mirror lies. Each one distorts. None reveals who she truly is.

HAGAR'S BROKEN MIRROR

Illustration by Mayah Welsh. Concept inspired by Charles Horton Cooley's sociological theory.

When we stand before a broken mirror, the shards reflect fragments of us, some real, some imagined. But never the whole truth. These fractured reflections drive Hagar into an identity crisis, one that mirrors the internal battles many of us face. She begins to believe she is what she has been through. Part of her wants to believe she is valuable, a solution to the couple's problem. But another part whispers that she is only a tool, destined to be used, abused, and discarded. She begins to ask the question so many of us fear to ask: Who am I? Am I loved or hated? Intelligent or insignificant? Worthy or worthless? A nameless slave, or someone's precious daughter?

For Hagar, it must have seemed like God did not see her, or if He did, she was left to wonder: *Who am I in the eyes of my master's God?* Does He notice a poor Egyptian girl, a foreigner caught in someone else's story? She has never heard the voice of the Lord, but has the Lord heard her cries? She has never seen God, but has God seen her? She knows she is part of Sarai's plan. She knows Abram is part of God's plan. But is she? Could someone like her, used, unseen, foreign, be part of the divine story?

These are valid questions, difficult, yes, but not unanswerable. At least not to the Lord. In the wilderness, far from the distorted mirrors of human judgment, a different reflection is waiting. Hagar doesn't see it yet, but she will. The moment is coming when she will meet the One who sees her (See chapter four), not as a function, not as property, but as a person. But first, the Lord will seek her. In that desolate place, running from the house of Abram, the father of faith, God, the Faithful Father, will find her. He will take the pen from Abram and Sarai and begin to edit her story.

WRITE
YOUR STORY

1. How has what you think others think about you shaped the way you see yourself?

2. How do Abram and Sarai refer to Hagar in Genesis 16, and what does that tell us about how they viewed her?

3. **Why is it unwise to base your self-worth on how you think others see you?**

4. How can you begin to use these Scriptures, "In the image of God He created them" (Genesis 1:27) and "I am fearfully and wonderfully made" (Psalm 139:14), to reshape how you see yourself in light of how God sees you?

WRITE YOUR PRAYER

Take a moment to speak to God about what you've just read and written. What do you need to say to Him? What do you want to ask or surrender? Use the space below to write your own prayer, from your heart to His.

3

FOUND BY THE FAITHFUL FATHER

Pregnant and alone, Hagar found herself in the desert. Her escape cost Abram a second wife and a son (yet to be born), and it cost Sarai a servant, but it cost Hagar her home. And yet, even there, homeless and vulnerable, she felt a strange sense of emotional relief. Still, she was likely physically exhausted, worn down by a journey longer than she was ever meant to endure.[23] She fled toward freedom, yet found herself imprisoned by the silence of solitude. Just her and the unborn child, to whom she could speak, but from whom she could not yet hear. She went missing. But the narrator keeps us in the dark as to whether she was missed. There is no mention of Abram or Sarai searching for her. But the Angel of the Lord sought her and found her by a well (Genesis 16:7).

The Angel of the Lord is widely understood to be the Lord Himself, as He speaks in the first person and with divine authority. Later, His appearance is often attributed with God. With this line of thought, Hagar had her own theophany.[24] That means God reveals and manifests Himself to her. Ironically, while living in the household of Abram, the friend of God and father of faith, Hagar had never encountered God. But in the wilderness, the Lord met her. Alone, desperate, and unseen, far from the covenant, far from the patriarch, and far from home, but she was not far from God's presence. This merciful encounter teaches us that while there is only one way to God, through Jesus Christ (John 14:6), God can reach us in many ways. He can meet the king in his palace, the poor in his need, the righteous in his devotion, and the sinner in his brokenness. Here, He met Hagar, in the desert.

---

[23] Henry M. Morris, *The Genesis Record: A Scientific and Devotional Commentary on the Book of Beginnings* (Grand Rapids: Baker Book House, 1976), Kindle ed., 459.

[24] W. Sibley Towner, *Genesis*, Westminster Bible Companion (Louisville: Westminster John Knox Press, 2001), 160.

The setting of this encounter, near a well, demands further reflection. In Biblical narratives, wells and springs often serve as "places of blessings" and "divine appointment," where destinies are shaped[25] (Genesis 24:11; 29:2; Exodus. 2:15). Usually, in well encounters in the Old Testament, husbands find their future wives, but in this encounter the Lord found Hagar. Whether there is a connection or not, it's worth noting that later in John 4, Jesus would find the Samaritan woman, an outcast, by a well. Like Hagar, she was a woman on the margins, yet she was seen, spoken to, and transformed by the encounter.

Later, while Jesus was in the desert fasting for forty days, He met the devil, the one who came to tempt Him (Matthew 4:1–11; Luke 4:1–13). But in our deserts, our places of wilderness, we don't meet the devil; we meet God, just as Hagar met God. The desert, in Scripture, is often a place of encounter, not just emptiness. Moses met God in the wilderness through a burning bush (Exodus 3:1–4). Elijah, exhausted and despairing, heard God's gentle whisper on Mount Horeb after fleeing into the desert (1 Kings 19:3–13). God may not have placed us in the desert, but He uses it, not to tempt us, but to try us, to shape us, and to make us better.

GOD KNOWS HAGAR'S NAME AND HER SITUATION

"The Angel of the Lord said, 'Hagar, slave of Sarai…'" (Genesis 16:8). Here God indeed did what Abram and Sarai omitted; He called her by name! Bible scholars have not reached a consensus on the meaning of her name. Some propose that *Hagar* may

---

[25] *Tremper Longman III and David E. Garland, eds., The Expositor's Bible Commentary: Genesis–Leviticus,* Revised Edition, vol. 1 (Grand Rapids: Zondervan, 2008), 176.

mean "fugitive," "foreigner," or "to dwell."[26] In Scripture, names are rarely random, they often reflect one's origin, circumstances, or destiny.[27] However, in Hagar's story, the exact meaning of her name is ultimately less important than the fact that God calls her by name. In a home where she had been unnamed and unseen, God's voice affirms her identity, not just as a servant, but as a person who is known, acknowledged, and worthy of being addressed.

We can imagine Hagar having a flashback to the last time she heard her name spoken, perhaps by her father back in Egypt, before her identity was reduced to that of a slave girl. Though Abram is honored as the father of all, in the beginning of this story he does not act as one, not to her, and not to her unborn child. He is portrayed as a husband who favors his first wife, Sarai, and dismissed his second wife, Hagar, and a distant father figure in the life growing inside Hagar. In the wilderness, the text presents us with two orphans: Hagar, whose father is never named, and her unborn son, whose father is notably absent. To reiterate, she is never named by the characters in the story, but here, she is called by her Heavenly Father first by her name. In that moment the author presents God as the Father of all (Malachi 2:10).

It would have been enough for the Lord to simply call her, "Hagar." But the Lord adds, "slave of Sarai." The inclusion of the Hebrew word *shiphchath Sarai*, "female slave of Sarai," raises a question: Why would God refer to her by the very role she is fleeing? Many of us don't want to be reminded of the labels we've been given, especially the ones tied to our pain, our past, or our place of shame. The truth is, while we may not want to be defined by our pain, it's even more harmful when others pretend it

---

[26] David W. Cotter, *Berit Olam: Studies in Hebrew Narrative and Poetry*, (Collegeville, MN: Liturgical Press, 2003), 103.

[27] Jeff A. Benner, *His Name Is One: An Ancient Hebrew Perspective of the Names of God* (College Station, TX: Virtualbookworm Publishing, 2003), 8–9.

doesn't exist. The Lord chose not to ignore Hagar's pain. So, He mentions both her name and her status intentionally. It shows that God not only knows her name, but also sees her condition.[28] He acknowledges both who she is and what she has endured.

THE QUESTION SHE COULD NOT ANSWER

After calling Hagar's name, the Angel of the Lord asks her two questions, one about her **origin**, the other about her **destiny**.[29] "Where have you come from," and "Where are you going?" To the first question, she responds: "I'm running away from my mistress Sarai."

Most of us, perhaps everyone, can relate to Hagar's succinct yet deeply honest answer, since many of us are running from something too: a painful past, a broken home, an abusive relationship, or a burden too heavy to bear. In Hagar's cry, we find our own voice. This is the first time she speaks in the narrative. In Abram's household, Hagar was nameless and voiceless. But in the wilderness, where everything else is stripped away, her name is spoken and her voice is finally heard. Contrary to her silent suffering, here her pain and desperation break through in speech. Though the wilderness seems desolate, it becomes a sacred space, a safe place to express sorrow, even if she doesn't yet understand who is listening. Only later will she come to realize that she is speaking to the *"God who hears"* (Genesis 16:11).

The second question "Where are you going?" is left without an answer because "Hagar did not know where she was going."[30] That's the exhausting part of running away. While we may know

---

[28] Zucker and Reiss, *The Matriarchs of Genesis*, 92.

[29] Phyllis Trible, *Texts of Terror: Literary-Feminist Readings of Biblical Narratives* (Philadelphia: Fortress Press, 1984), 15.

[30] Stanley M. Horton, ed., *The Complete Biblical Library: Old Testament – Genesis*, vol. 1 (Springfield, MO: World Library Press, Inc., 1994), 133.

whom or what we are running from, we don't always know to whom or to what we are running. And yet, it is often in that not knowing, when our direction is unclear and our future feels out of reach, that God, through His mercy, finds us. It is there, in the wilderness of uncertainty, that God begins to shape our destiny. But before Hagar can move forward, she is given a command that seems to take her a step back, a return to the very place she fled.

WHY DID GOD SEND HAGAR BACK TO WHAT SHE ESCAPED?

Then, the Angel of the Lord told Hagar, "Go back to your mistress and submit to her" (Genesis 16:9). This command in the dialogue between Hagar and the Angel is difficult to read. When running away from abuse, violence, and mistreatment, it is rarely advisable for the oppressed to return to their perpetrator or re-enter the cycle.[31] Hence the reader may wonder why would a merciful God, instead of rescuing a vulnerable woman from mistreatment and enslavement, command her to return to her jealous and merciless mistress?

The question becomes even more pressing when comparing God's command to Hagar with the protections later prescribed in the Mosaic Law regarding runaway slaves. As Paul Copan notes in his book, *Is God a Moral Monster?*, in Deuteronomy God declares, "You shall not give up to his master a slave who has escaped from his master to you" (Deuteronomy 23:15 ESV).[32] The text implies that when an enslaved person flees, the community is called to become a place of refuge, refusing to send them

---

[31] Lynn Japinga, *Preaching the Women of the Old Testament: Who They Were and Why They Matter* (Louisville: Westminster John Knox Press, 2017), 14, ProQuest Ebook Central,

[32] Paul Copan, *Is God a Moral Monster? Making Sense of the Old Testament God* (Grand Rapids, MI: Baker Books, 2011), 63, Kindle.

back into the oppression of slavery. At first glance, the instruction God gives to Hagar seems inconsistent with His character, as
He is known for siding with the oppressed. Yet when we consider
Hagar's current situation more closely, we begin to see that there
may be several beneficial reasons why God would instruct her to
return to her mistress.

The first, perhaps the most probable, reason is survival concern. The young pregnant Hagar had no provision for her journey. Even later, in Genesis 21, when she was sent away with basic
supplies, bread and water, it still took divine intervention to save
her and her son. They were dying of thirst in the wilderness, and
it was only the power of God that opened Hagar's eyes to the well
that sustained their lives. So, in this earlier instance, as much as
she longed for freedom and emancipation, it was probably not
the right time nor the right method, and the Lord knew it. James
McKeown rightly notes that the mission to go back to her native
land "was impossible" and that is why the Angel of the Lord sent
her back.[33] It is reasonable to conclude that God's instruction
may have been as much about preserving life as it was about
anything else.

Another reason could be that, perhaps the one that offers the
most relief and softens the tension in this difficult story, is found
in the Hebrew word used when God tells Hagar to return. The
Hebrew word translated "submit" (*vehit'anni*) can also carry the
sense of "taking a posture of humility."[34] It doesn't necessarily
mean to accept abuse, but rather to adopt a posture of humility.
This shifts the tone of the command; it's not about endorsing oppression. But God wanted Hagar to honor Sarai as the first wife
instead of taking advantage of her insecurity. This interpretation
is further supported by the fact that, after Hagar's return, the text

---

[33] James McKeown, *Genesis, The Two Horizons Old Testament Commentary*
(Grand Rapids: Eerdmans, 2008), 97.

[34] Horton, *Genesis*, 133.

no longer describes any mistreatment from Sarai. While another conflict arises years later (Genesis 21), it centers on inheritance, not abuse.

The final reason could be, as Philemon Ibrahim notes, maybe God intended to show Hagar that one of the ways He strengthens the oppressed to endure humiliation, demotion, and suffering is not by immediately removing them from hardship, but by giving them the grace to endure it.[35] In this, Hagar is invited to take comfort in the truth that God's grace is sufficient, not just for survival, but for perseverance in the midst of affliction.

IF YOU CAN COUNT THE SAND OF THE DESERT, YOU CAN COUNT HAGAR'S DESCENDANTS

In the Abram narrative, God's call to "Go" (Genesis 12:1) is indeed paired with a promise, "I will make you a great nation." Similarly, in Hagar's story, God gives her a command ("Go back to your mistress") but also attaches a promise: "I will increase your descendants so much that they will be too numerous to count" (Genesis 16:10). Later, God confirmed this promise to Abram (Genesis 17:20).[36] Then the Angel of the Lord announced the birth of her child with a familiar structure: "You are now pregnant and you will give birth to a son…" (Genesis 16:11).

This divine announcement mirrors the pattern seen in other significant birth narratives, such as Samson (Judges 13:5), the prophecy of the Messiah (Isaiah 7:14), and the angel's message to Mary (Luke 1:31).[37] Then the Lord revealed the child's name:

---

[35] Philemon Ibrahim, "How Heartless Is the Mistress of Hagar?: Hagar, the Used and Rejected Egyptian Slave," *Journal of Biblical Theology* 6, no. 2 (2023): 244.

[36] *The Complete Biblical Library: Old Testament Study Bible*, edited by Thoralf Gilbrant (Springfield, MO: World Library Press, 1994), 133.

[37] Bill T. Arnold, *Genesis*, New Cambridge Bible Commentary (Cambridge: Cambridge University Press, 2009), 165.

"You shall name him Ishmael, for the LORD has heard of your misery" (Genesis 16:11), and his destiny; "He will be a wild donkey of a man" (Genesis 16:12). This is a striking revelation about the type of freedom that Ishmael will experience. One can visualize a donkey running in the dessert and without any fear of being oppressed. In the same way, this passage is to be understood as Ishmael inheriting his mother's fierce desire for freedom.[38] But unlike Hagar, Ishmael would not live as a slave; he would be a free man, "roaming the desert on his own terms."[39] Due to his refusal to be a slave, Ishmael would live in constant conflict with those who try to dominate him (Genesis 16:12).

This prophecy does not seem to be a curse, it's a comfort. It reassures Hagar that her son will never be mistreated as she was, and he will never be subjected to the cruelty of a master or mistress. His very name affirms this hope: *Ishmael*, "God hears." God heard Hagar's cry in her misery and responded with a promise of freedom for the son of the slave. And in that moment, Hagar knows something even more profound: the child they considered a mistake is not a mistake in God's eyes. He carries his own destiny. He will have his own story. It is almost as if Hagar and Ishmael, here in the early patriarchal narrative, are closer to Jochebed and Moses than even to Abram and Sarai. Empowered by this truth, Hagar returns, not as a broken woman, but as a mother whose son is here on purpose.[40]

---

[38] *The Complete Biblical Library: Old Testament Study Bible*, edited by Thoralf Gilbrant (Springfield, MO: World Library Press, 1994), 133.

[39] James McKeown, *Genesis*, The Two Horizons Old Testament Commentary (Grand Rapids: Eerdmans, 2008), 97.

[40] Victor P. Hamilton, *The Book of Genesis: Chapters 1–17*, The New International Commentary on the Old Testament (Grand Rapids, MI: Eerdmans, 1990), 455.

WRITE
YOUR STORY

*You're invited to pause, reflect, and even journal as you go,
because this isn't just Hagar's story; it's yours too!*

1. This chapter reminds us that God can find us in unexpected places. What does that tell you about God? And if applicable, where were you and what was your life like when Jesus found you?

2. Wells in Scripture are often places where men meet their future wives, like Rebekah (Genesis 24) and Zipporah (Exodus 2). What made Hagar's well encounter different, and how does it compare to the Samaritan woman's meeting with Jesus in John 4?

3. **Describe a season in your life when you were running from something without knowing where you were going, and God met you there.**

4. When life gets overwhelming, how can you choose to run into the arms of God instead of staying busy, getting distracted, or running away?

WRITE YOUR PRAYER

Take a moment to speak to God about what you've just read and written. What do you need to say to Him? What do you want to ask or surrender? Use the space below to write your own prayer from your heart to His.

4

EL ROI: THE GOD WHO SEES ME

This epiphany in the desert was not Hagar's pursuit of God, but God's pursuit of her. It was God who found her, called her by name, and named her child. Hagar simply responded to the loving pursuit of God, and she named the Lord "the One who sees me." This follows the consistent pattern of Scripture: God initiates, and humanity responds. Notice, this is the only time in Scripture that someone "male or female" names God.[41] This moment was so profound that some feminist scholars have called Hagar a theologian in her own right.[42]

What we typically see in Scripture concerning the name of God is that people either name a place in honor of what God has done, such as Abram, who named the mountain "The Lord Will Provide" (*Yahweh Jireh*) after God provided a ram in place of Isaac for the sacrifice (Genesis 22:14) or God reveals His own name directly, as He did to Abram in Genesis 17:1, saying, "I am El Shaddai" (*Ani El Shaddai*), meaning "God Almighty," or better translated, "God-the-Mountain-One." But in Hagar's story, something extraordinary happens: God does not reveal His name to her, yet she boldly gives Him a name. This is a sacred and singular moment in the entire Biblical narrative. This privileged act should be understood as Hagar's way of personalizing her experience with God.[43] While it is risky to base our theology solely on personal experience, our theology must still be experienced because we worship a living God. Here, Hagar pioneers that truth in the only way she knows how, by calling God *El Roi*, "the God who sees [her]" (Genesis 16:13).

---

[41] The Jewish Publication Society, *Etz Hayim: Torah and Commentary*, ed. David L. Lieber et al. (Philadelphia: Jewish Publication Society, 2001), 18.

[42] Phyllis Trible, *Texts of Terror: Literary-Feminist Readings of Biblical Narratives*, 40th Anniversary Edition (Minneapolis: Fortress Press, 2022), 18.

[43] Bill T. Arnold, *Genesis*, New Cambridge Bible Commentary (Cambridge: Cambridge University Press, 2009), 165.

Though naming was traditionally a privilege of the one in authority,[44] like a father naming a daughter, Hagar's naming of God is not a breach of theological order, but an expression of deep reverence and gratitude. Hagar knows the power of being called by name, something her master and mistress failed to do. But God did, and in that moment, she tasted what it meant to be seen and known, not just by anyone, but by God Himself. For Hagar, names matter. She realizes that in the desert, everyone has a name: she is Hagar, her son is Ishmael, both named aloud. But the God who named her child has not revealed His own name to her. So, she does something bold, something unheard of in the Biblical story up to this point, yet something meaningful. She names God. Now, in this sacred moment in the wilderness, no one is unnamed. Not even God. The author does not tell us how God responded to Hagar, a marginalized woman and slave, who named Him, but the silence suggests that God did not correct her, but received it.[45]

HAGAR IS SEEN

It is not known whether Hagar wrote *El Roi* in the sand that day, but what is certain is this: *El Roi* would always be written on her heart. The revelation was so dear to her that she did not merely name God, she also named the place: "the well of the Living One who sees me" (*Beer-lahai-roi*), following the more traditional pattern of honoring a superior by naming a place after them (Genesis 16:13–14).[46] Yet both names, God's and the well's, point to the same reality: Hagar is seen by God.

[44] Lynn Japinga, *Preaching the Women of the Old Testament: Who They Were and Why They Matter* (Louisville: Westminster John Knox Press, 2017), 14, ProQuest Ebook Central.

[45] Tammi J. Schneider, *Mothers of Promise: Women in the Book of Genesis*, (Grand Rapids: Baker Academic, 2008), 110.

[46] R. Kent Hughes, *Genesis: Beginning and Blessing*, Preaching the Word (Wheaton, IL: Crossway, 2004), 243.

In the famous words of David in Psalm 139, we are invited to ask, "Where can Hagar hide or flee from the presence of the God who sees?" If she goes up to the heavens or down into the wilderness, *El Roi* is there. Even the obscurity of the desert is not dark to the God who sees. This is what separates the living God from all others. He has eyes, and He sees not only our strength, but our sorrow; not only our public worship, but our private weeping. John Goldingay puts it well: "The difference between the nation's gods and [our God] is not that the false gods have body parts but [our God] is spiritual. It is that [our God] has body parts that work."[47] In other words, our God has eyes and He saw Hagar's suffering, He sees ours, too.

NOW HAGAR SEES

Hagar was not only seen, but she also saw. As the verse suggests, "She [has] now seen the One who sees [her]" (Genesis 16:13). When we realize that we are seen by God, we always receive a new vision. It is then that we begin to see ourselves as He sees us. Paul echoes this truth in 2 Corinthians 3:16–18, when he writes, "When one turns to the Lord, the veil is removed. And as we behold the Lord, like looking into a mirror, we are transformed into His image, from glory to glory." Here, Hagar's veil of shame, embarrassment, and guilt is removed. She now stands, not before the broken mirror Abram and Sarai had crafted for her, where her reflection was partial and distorted, but before a mirror she had not yet known, the one shaped by God. In it, she sees clearly. She now sees herself through God's eyes. More than a slave, she is a daughter, mother of a multitude, and a woman with a divine purpose.

---

[47] John Goldingay, *Psalms, Volume 3: Psalms 90–150*, Baker Commentary on the Old Testament Wisdom and Psalms, ed. Tremper Longman III (Grand Rapids, MI: Baker Academic, 2008), 331.

While it's uncertain whether the phrase "seeing God" should be taken literally in Genesis 16:13, the possibility invites careful reflection. On one hand, Scripture affirms that "No one can see [God] and live" (Exodus 33:20), and yet, no death is recorded in response to Hagar's vision. If Hagar did, in some sense, see God, then she saw only the dimension of His presence that she could bear. God's grace is not only that He reveals Himself, but that He restrains His glory to protect those He loves. His *kabod*, His weight, His glory, is mercifully measured out for mere humans.

This same mercy was granted to Jacob, who, after wrestling with God, named the place *Peniel*, saying, "It is because I saw God face to face, and yet my life was spared." (Genesis 32:30). Even Moses, in his bold request, "Show me Your glory" (Exodus 33:18), was only granted a partial glimpse. God hid him in the cleft of the rock, covered him with His hand, and allowed him to see only His back, while proclaiming His goodness and unfailing love. Here, God graciously protected Moses, too.

While debates continue regarding whether this theophany, Hagar's, as well as others in Scripture were literal or metaphorical, such questions are not the only lens through which we engage the text. As we read this passage, we are invited to hold on to a deeper truth: just as it is true that no one can see God and live, it is equally true that no one sees God and remains the same.

She Saw God, Now She Sees Her Baby Boy

Genesis 16 concludes with these verses: "So Hagar bore Abram a son, and Abram gave the name Ishmael to the son she had borne. Abram was eighty-six years old when Hagar bore him Ishmael" (Genesis 16:15–16). Notice that Abram names the child Ishmael, the very name the Lord had given to Hagar in the wilderness, which suggests that the patriarch had become aware of her encounter with God.[48] Or, she told Abram that she met his God and He is gracious and good, something God's people often fail to display.

At the beginning of the chapter, Hagar is introduced as an Egyptian slave given to the couple by Pharaoh. But by the end, she is part of Abram's household, not because of human arrangement, but because God sent her back, and she obeyed. Now, however, the family dynamic has grown tense. Hagar has returned, but she has already drawn a boundary; she will not tolerate mistreatment and is prepared to flee again if necessary. Hagar is no longer just pregnant; she has given birth to Abram's firstborn son and Abram accepted the son and even named him. Could the son they carefully planned as the solution to God's promise become the very source of the conflict within their family? To this question, we now turn.

---

[48] R. Kent Hughes, *Genesis: Beginning and Blessing*, Preaching the Word (Wheaton, IL: Crossway, 2004), 243.

WRITE
YOUR STORY

*You're invited to pause, reflect, and even journal as you go,
because this isn't just Hagar's story; it's yours too!*

1. If you were to give God a name based on how He has shown up in your life, what would it be, and why?

2. How does the name El Roi, the name Hagar gave to God in Genesis 16:13, differ from other names like El Shaddai (Genesis 17:1) or Yahweh Jireh (Genesis 22:14)?

3. What makes Hagar's naming of God unique compared to names that were revealed by God Himself or given in honor of a place?

4. When you have an encounter with God, or come to know Him in a way you never have before, how can you continually remember those moments so that you don't lose sight of them?

WRITE YOUR PRAYER

Take a moment to speak to God about what you've just read and written. What do you need to say to Him? What do you want to ask or surrender? Use the space below to write your own prayer, from your heart to His.

5

THE BLESSING ON THE OTHER SIDE OF REJECTION

In chapter 17, the Lord appeared to Abram when he was nine-ty-nine years old and revealed His name to the patriarch as *El Shaddai*, "God Almighty" (Genesis 17:1). The author uses the final verse of Genesis 16 and the opening of Genesis 17 to provide key chronological details. Abram was eighty-six years old when Ishmael was born (Genesis 16:16) and ninety-nine at the start of chapter 17 (Genesis 17:1). Thirteen years passed between the birth of his first son through Hagar and the Lord's next re-corded appearance. The purpose of this appearance was for God to renew the covenant and reaffirm His promise to Abram. Un-like the initial promise in Genesis 12, which focused on land, this renewal emphasizes the promise of descendants. For the first time, Abram is told specifically that the promised child will come through Sarai. The Lord says, "I will bless [your wife Sarai] and will surely give you a son by her" (Genesis 17:16). It is at that moment that Abram realized he had misunderstood God's ulti-mate plan and timeline. His and Sarai's earlier attempt to fulfill the promise on their own was premature and fell short of God's plan.

God, in His gracious nature, never fails to lift up the soul of a person who has recognized their mistakes, shortcomings, and imperfections. In this passage, the Lord proceeds to change the patriarch's name from "Abram" to "Abraham," meaning "father of many nations" (Genesis 17:6). This new name reassures Abra-ham that, despite his detour in faith, God's promises still stand. As Paul reminds us, "If we are faithless, He remains faithful" (2 Timothy 2:13). God also changes Sarai's name to "Sarah," con-firming that she, not Hagar, will bear the covenant child and become the mother of nations. Do these name changes signal a new Abraham and a new Sarah? Perhaps not entirely new, but certainly renewed. These name changes suggest a new, yet still imperfect, Abraham and Sarah.

WHEN THE SOLUTION BECOMES THE PROBLEM

In Genesis 21, as the Lord had promised, Abraham (now one hundred years old) and Sarah (around ninety) finally receive their long-awaited son. He is the child of promise. With his birth, Sarah's social status shifts. She is no longer just the beloved wife, but now a mother, and not just any mother, but rather the mother of the covenant child. The text does not tell us how Hagar responded or whether she felt insecure now that the one thing she had once provided, offspring, her mistress also possessed. If she had once looked upon Sarah with contempt, as described in Genesis 16, that posture could no longer be sustained. However, we are not left in the dark about what Ishmael, the son of Hagar, now around sixteen years old, thought of Isaac, the son of the promise.

When Isaac was weaned, likely around the age of three (that was the age children were traditionally weaned) Abraham held a party for him.[49] On that day of celebration, Ishmael laughed at his little brother instead rejoicing with him. In fact, the Hebrew word for laughter in this verse can be translated as "mocking," which means, the laugh was not one of joy.[50]

While such an act must never be excused or encouraged, it invites us to consider the underlying emotions behind such jealousy. In Genesis 21, a feast is held for the younger brother, Isaac, but no celebration is mentioned for Ishmael. This dynamic is echoed in Jesus' parable of the prodigal son, where the older brother refuses to join the feast for his younger sibling. The older son protests, not because the feast is wrong, but because he feels overlooked.[51]

---

[49] Hughes, Genesis: Beginning and Blessing, 242.

[50] *The Complete Biblical Library: Old Testament – Genesis*, ed. Thoralf Gilbrant (Springfield, MO: World Library Press, 1994), 177.

[51] James McKeown, *Genesis*, The Two Horizons Old Testament Commentary (Grand Rapids: Eerdmans, 2008), 114.

Regardless of the underlying reason, this kind of behavior is not tolerated in the house of Abraham, even Sarah shows neither the patience nor the grace to endure such mockery. Sarah urges Abraham, "Get rid of that slave woman and her son…" (Genesis 21:10). Sarah's command is harsh, but her anger is triggered by what she interprets as a threat to her son, the promised heir. The consequences are immediate, and they fall not only on Ishmael, but on Hagar as well. Some commentators deem Sarah's action as unrighteous.[52] Rightly so, since the second part of verse 10 reveals the hidden agenda of Sarah, that is she does not want "Ishmael to share in the inheritance with [her] son Isaac" (Genesis 21:6). Even if Abraham prays that God blesses Ishmael, this is not the prayer of his wife. Sarah's concern is entirely for her biological son, not the adopted one.

By now, Abraham has spent sixteen years learning how to be a father, one who loves his children deeply, even when they fall short. Unlike earlier moments when he simply agreed with Sarah's requests, this time his fatherly instinct rises. He cannot bring himself to send his son away, as Sarah has asked. "The matter distressed Abraham greatly" because as a father, he is responsible to provide, to protect, and to love his children (Genesis 21:11). While Ishmael's behavior may have been wrong, Abraham believes that the solution is not to cast him out. Ishmael may have failed, but he still belongs. Father Abraham knows that sons and daughters, despite their shortcomings, long to hear from their parents that they are still loved and belong. So, Abraham does not initially agree with Sarah.

Now, considering that it was the Lord who had once sent Hagar back, the reader expects God to speak again, this time about whether Ishmael should be expelled. Yes, God did intervene. But He does not settle the matter in the way we expect.

---

[52] Hughes, *Genesis: Beginning and Blessing*, 242.

Instead, He answers according to a bigger plan. The Lord told Abraham to "listen to whatever Sarah tells [him]" Because Isaac is the promised heir (Genesis 21:12). This was the first time God asked Abraham to sacrifice a son, not with a knife, but with separation. As we read this melancholic part of the story, we may find ourselves just as confused as Hagar was, perhaps even upset with God, maybe disappointed. We might ask why would God send Hagar back to a place He knew would ultimately reject her? Why would He encourage her return, only to permit her expulsion? Or perhaps, this rejection is not the end. Perhaps it serves a greater purpose, one that neither Hagar nor we can yet see.

ONCE A RUNAWAY, NOW HAGAR AND ISHMAEL ARE SENT AWAY

In his distress, Abraham chooses to obey God, even though he does not fully understand God's decision. "Early the next morning," Abraham rises and says goodbye to Hagar and the boy (Genesis 21:14). Abraham's faith shows up most clearly when his understanding runs out. Since later, when God would ask him to offer up Isaac, Abraham would trust that God could raise his son from the dead; therefore, he was ready to sacrifice his son (Hebrews 11:19). So here, it is understandable to assume that Abraham reasoned that if he, as an earthly father and cares this deeply for his son Ishmael, how much more will God, the heavenly Father, know how to protect and provide for him? (cf. Matthew 7:11). But the same cannot be assumed for the victims. Hagar and Ishmael do not know God the way Abraham does. What they know is this: they've been cast out by the people of God, and God said nothing to stop it. Abraham is walking by faith; they are walking in rejection and abandonment.

With a heavy heart, Hagar and Ishmael set out the next morning, heading back into the desert. But this time, the journey isn't her decision, it's her mistress's. Some have noted, "In chapter 16, Hagar ran away. In chapter 21, Hagar and Ishmael are sent away."[53] With each step, the house where they were no longer welcome fades behind them. Perhaps they look back, but they cannot return. That's the sad part of rejection; you want to stay, but you're not welcome. You want to belong, but you're not chosen. You want to be seen, but you remain invisible.

A Journey with Little to No Supply

The first time Hagar fled into the desert, no provision for her journey is mentioned. But this time, "early the next morning Abraham took some food and a skin of water and gave them to Hagar" (Genesis 21:14). Yet even here, the supplies were not enough. As a wealthy man, Abraham could have sent her off with servants, camels, or ample goods, but the text offers no explanation for his minimal provision. One possibility is that Abraham expected Hagar and Ishmael to take refuge in a nearby settlement, not to journey far into the wilderness.[54] But the journey did not go as Abraham may have planned. Hagar "went on her way and wandered in the Desert of Beersheba" (Genesis 21:14), and soon, the limited supplies ran out. When the water she carried ran out, Hagar placed the boy, then about sixteen years old, under one of the bushes, unable to bear the sight of her son dying (Genesis 21:15–16). In that moment, perhaps she wished she could hand Ishmael back to his adoptive mother Sarah, someone with more resources, more power. But even if the thought crossed her mind, she could not afford to make the journey back. And even if she could, Sarah no longer needed the boy now that she had a son of her own.

---

[53] Daniel C. Juster, "Ishmael and the Blessing of Abraham," in *Perspectives on Our Father Abraham: Essays in Honor of Marvin R. Wilson*, ed. Steven A. Hunt (Grand Rapids: Eerdmans, 2010), 346.

[54] Juster, "Ishmael and the Blessing of Abraham," 347.

Does Hagar wonder if she has failed as a biological mother? Is she blaming herself? The narrative offers us no grounds to place blame on her for Ishmael's suffering. In fact, it presents a portrait of a mother who has done everything within her power. When she fled the first time, she obeyed God's command and returned, entrusting her child to a home where her mistress could care for him better than she could alone. And now, in the wilderness, there is no trace of selfishness in her actions. Even as her strength fails, she gently shelters the boy beneath a bush, not only to protect him from the heat of the sun, but perhaps to spare him from seeing her tears, and to spare herself from watching him die. The text indeed says that she sat at a distance, "for she thought, 'I cannot watch the boy die.' And as she sat there, she began to sob" (Genesis 21:16). Ishmael's name reminds us that God hears. But the question remains: does He hear even when we're too broken to pray, when all we can do is sob?

REJECTED BY GOD'S PEOPLE, BUT ACCEPTED BY GOD

The next verse immediately answers what we might otherwise question: God does hear our cries, even when they have no words. Verse 17 says, "God heard the boy crying." In Genesis 16:11, God heard Hagar's misery. In Genesis 17:20, God heard Abraham's plea on behalf of Ishmael. And now, in the wilderness, God hears the boy himself. It could mean that the author intends to present an unwavering truth about our compassionate God. That is, God hears women (Hagar); God hears men (Abraham); God hears children or adolescents too (Ishmael). Or maybe the author emphasizes that God heard the boy to draw attention to the fact that Hagar never cried out to God. Her silence is striking. The woman who once named the Lord *El Roi* does not even call upon His name when she is in distress. It's ironic. Has she forgotten? Or does she wonder if He has forgotten her? Was she so rejected by God's people that she assumed she had been rejected by God Himself? Anne Graham Lotz in her book, *Wounded by God's People*, encourages us to remember that our relationship with God must be strong enough, and our understanding of His Word deep enough, to know this truth: "Being rejected by [God's people] does not mean being rejected by [God]."[55] This is a truth that God will soon confirm to Hagar.

Unexpectedly, Hagar hears a familiar voice, the voice of the Angel of the Lord. He says, "Do not be afraid; God has heard the boy crying as he lies there. Lift the boy up and take him by the hand, for I will make him into a great nation" (Genesis 21:17–18). The reaffirmation of the promise is a divine hint that the boy will not die. Then the Angel of the Lord "opened her eyes and she saw a well of water. So, she went and filled the skin with water and gave the boy a drink" (Genesis 21:19). The story ends with a stunning intervention: God opened Hagar's eyes to the well that was already near her. First, she receives a renewed vision of God's provision and then a reaffirmation that she has not been rejected by heaven. In fact, the very next verse says, "God was with the boy as he grew up" (Genesis 21:20). God's intervention is evident here, but why didn't He prevent their rejection from Abraham's household in the first place?

FREE INDEED

To begin answering this question, we must first acknowledge two key truths in the story. First, although Hagar returned to Abraham's household in obedience to God, that does not mean she no longer desired freedom. Obedience did not erase her longing. And second, God's plan for Ishmael was never for him to remain in Abraham's house. From the beginning, God had promised him

---

[55] Anne Graham Lotz, *Wounded by God's People: Discovering How God's Love Heals Our Hearts* (Nashville: W Publishing Group, 2013), 116.

a future of his own, with his own blessing and his own freedom. So perhaps a better question than "Why did God allow Hagar to be rejected *from the very place He sent her?*" is this: Could it be that God wanted her freedom to be recognized, legally and permanently, according to the laws of the time?

Since Ishmael was Abraham's first born, though by a servant, he would have been considered the legal heir by both adoption and birth order. According to ancient custom, the firstborn held the right to a double portion of the inheritance. This principle is reflected later in the story of Esau and Jacob, where Esau, the firstborn, gives up his birthright and ultimately loses the blessing (Genesis 25:29–34; 27:36). Sarah was afraid that would be the case. She devised her own plan to prevent Ishmael from enjoying the birthright. Since Sarah knows that the ancient legal codes of that time stated that once someone becomes free, they have forfeited their claim to inheritance, she forced Abraham to free Hagar and Ishmael.[56]

The author of Genesis gives us a hint of this in the reason Sarah gave for the expulsion of Hagar and her son: "Get rid of that slave woman and her son, for that woman's son will never share in the inheritance with my son Isaac" (Genesis 21:10). In this demand, Sarah saw Isaac's future. Abraham saw the rejection of his son and Hagar. But God saw something else, freedom. In a way, Sarah was right: Ishmael would not share in the inheritance with Isaac. But not because he was rejected; rather, because God had His own plan for Ishmael. As a free man, he would receive his own inheritance, his own future, and his own blessing, just as God had promised to his mother and father (Genesis 16:10; 17:20; 21:13, 21:18).

------

[56] Stephen J. Binz, *Abraham: Father of All Believers* (Collegeville, MN: Liturgical Press, 2005), 74.

It is encouraging to see that God can edit our rejections and make them work for our good (Romans 8:28). When Jesus was rejected by His own people, God used that very moment to open the door for "whosoever believes in Him." As John writes,

> He came to that which was his own, but his own did not receive him. Yet to all who did receive him, to those who believed in his name, he gave the right to become children of God (John 1:11–12).

This is not to downplay the pain of rejection, but to acknowledge that God often sees collateral blessings in what we call losses. Beyond being rejected by that specific university, God saw connections and growth waiting for you elsewhere. Even when you were let go from the job that supported your family, on the other side of that unfortunate situation, God saw a place for you, a place where your purpose would go beyond monetary compensation. When you were not loved back, God saw an opportunity to awaken your awareness of His love for you, and to teach you the value of loving yourself. The list could go on. But this much is clear: God sees the bigger picture, especially when we don't.

WRITE
YOUR STORY

*You're invited to pause, reflect, and even journal as you go,
because this isn't just Hagar's story; it's yours too!*

1. Describe a moment when you felt rejected or excluded. What made that moment stand out to you?

2. When Sarah wanted Hagar and Ishmael expelled (Genesis 21:9–21), what did God tell Abraham to do, and how did He comfort him in that moment?

3. How do you respond when rejection comes not from the world, but from God's own people, from those in the church? What emotions or thoughts rise up in you in those moments?

4. Since we've seen that God hears even the prayers we can't speak, how will you keep trusting him in moments when you don't have words?

WRITE YOUR PRAYER

Take a moment to speak to God about what you've just read and written. What do you need to say to Him? What do you want to ask or surrender? Use the space below to write your own prayer, from your heart to His.

6

THE BIGGER PICTURE

If you have made it this far in the story, then you have already realized that Hagar's journey is painful, yet redemptive in nature. At first glance, the Divine seems silent, yet He is never absent. Her story is as complex and uneven as life itself, filled with highs and lows, and we can't help but find ourselves caught in the emotional rollercoaster it evokes. We've walked with Hagar through deserts, silences, heartbreaks, mistreatment, abuse, and rejection, and we've shared in her moments of hope as well. At times, we have wept with her; at others, we have rejoiced. Like some of our stories, Hagar's journey has unfolded in ways we might have chosen to write differently. Now, as we come to the end, we must view Hagar's story through two distinct lenses: the strange and the divine.

First, the strange lens. Her story often feels bizarre and out of place, at times, even purposeless. She was a poor, foreign, nameless slave girl who became a wife, only to be demoted back to slavery. She fled into the desert alone and pregnant, with a child who was not truly her own, driven out by mistreatment. There, she was found by the Angel of the Lord, only to be sent back to the very house she had escaped. And after returning, she was eventually rejected again, cast out with her son into the wilderness, where thirst and hunger nearly claimed their lives.

Second, the divine lens. We have seen that when Abraham and Sarah did not even care to look for her, whether from their pasture or their home, the Angel of the Lord sought her out and found her. Like a good shepherd who leaves the ninety-nine to find the one lost sheep, He met her in the wilderness (Luke 15:4). Though in the house of the patriarch she was nameless and voiceless, the Lord called her by name and gave her a voice by entering into dialogue with her. In the words of Ephesians 2:12, Hagar was, at first, "a foreigner to the covenants of the promise, without hope and without God in the [wilderness]." Yet in the wilderness, she encountered God in her solitude, and received a promise of her own.

When Abraham, a good human father, was forced to send Hagar away, the water he gave her was so limited it could not sustain the full journey. But God, the Heavenly Father, opened her eyes and gave her access to a well. Through God's purpose and design, we see that although she began her journey as a slave girl carrying someone else's child, that child became her own, and she was granted her freedom. This is the mystery of her story, and ours: that what seems strange, God can make divine.

THE BIGGER PICTURE

It becomes even more compelling to realize that Hagar, who accidentally became part of Abraham's story, was purposely written into God's plan. For this, we must turn to Genesis 37:28, where we are told that it was the Ishmaelites, descendants of the matriarch, Hagar, whom God used to transport Joseph into Egypt, ultimately positioning him to save the world from famine.[57] One cannot help but notice that it is the descendants of the Egyptian slave, Hagar, who end up delivering into bondage Joseph, the descendant of the free woman, Sarah.[58]

While it may be tempting to draw conclusions about poetic justice or to suggest that no people group is immune from becoming either the oppressed or the oppressor, the text offers no indication of revenge. We must not assume that God orchestrat-

[57] Scholars differ on the identity of the Ishmaelites in Genesis 37. David W. Cotter distinguishes the Ishmaelites as Hagar's descendants and the Midianites as Keturah's. James McKeown notes the Midianites descended from Keturah and may have intermarried with the Ishmaelites. Bill T. Arnold sees the names as overlapping, while the *Cornerstone Biblical Commentary* identifies the Ishmaelites as direct descendants of Hagar.

[58] Allen P. Ross, *Genesis*, in *Cornerstone Biblical Commentary: Genesis and Exodus*, ed. Philip W. Comfort, vol. 1 (Carol Stream, IL: Tyndale House, 2008), 211.

ed the Ishmaelites to repay Sarah's descendants for past mistreatment. Rather, the point is this: God can redeem what humanity has mishandled. In this case, He uses the rejected and the abused to preserve not only Joseph's life but the lives of many. Through the descendants of Hagar, God makes a way for deliverance to come, transforming the rejected into the rescuers.

The way in which God entered Hagar's life as the Editor par excellence, revising the pain, shame, and mistreatment others had written into her story, reveals His redemptive nature. Even when God does not cause the chaos, He still enters it graciously. He edits what has been mishandled. The flow of redemption is this: What God does not prevent, He intervenes in, and what He does not intervene in, He redeems and makes it work together for our good, according to His divine purpose (Romans 8:28). This is not only true in Hagar's story, but also in ours. No matter how much ink has been spilled in your story and regardless of who the writers have been, take comfort in this: if your story feels strange, God's redemptive pen can make it divine. Yes, your life can be both strange and, yet, divine.

WRITE
YOUR STORY

You're invited to pause, reflect, and even journal as you go, because this isn't just Hagar's story; it's yours too!

1. If your life were a puzzle made up of both good and painful moments, what do you think the bigger picture might look like?

2. According to Genesis 37:28, whose descendants brought Joseph to Egypt?

3. Create a timeline of your life and identify key moments, especially those that felt strange, painful, or unexpected. Then, make note of where you now see God's hand at work in those moments. What seemed strange then, could it have been divine?

WRITE YOUR PRAYER

Take a moment to speak to God about what you've just read and written. What do you need to say to Him? What do you want to ask or surrender? Use the space below to write your own prayer, from your heart to His.

BIBLIOGRAPHY

Arnold, Bill T. *Genesis*. New Cambridge Bible Commentary. Cambridge: Cambridge University Press, 2009.

Binz, Stephen J. *Abraham: Father of All Believers*. Collegeville, MN: Liturgical Press, 2005.

Cooley, Charles Horton. *Human Nature and the Social Order*. New York: Scribner's, 1902.

Copan, Paul. *Is God a Moral Monster? Making Sense of the Old Testament God*. Grand Rapids, MI: Baker Books, 2011. Kindle.

Cotter, David W. *Genesis*. Berit Olam: Studies in Hebrew Narrative and Poetry. Collegeville, MN: Liturgical Press, 2003.

Gilbrant, Thoralf, ed. *The Complete Biblical Library: Old Testament – Genesis*. Springfield, MO: World Library Press, 1994.

Goldingay, John. *Psalms, Volume 3: Psalms 90–150*. Baker Commentary on the Old Testament Wisdom and Psalms. edited by Tremper Longman III. Grand Rapids, MI: Baker Academic, 2008.

Hartley, John E. *Genesis*. Vol. 1 of *New International Biblical Commentary*. Peabody, MA: Hendrickson Publishers, 2000.

Hughes, R. Kent. *Genesis: Beginning and Blessing*. Preaching the Word. Wheaton, IL: Crossway, 2004.

Ibrahim, Philemon. "How Heartless Is the Mistress of Hagar?: Hagar, the Used and Rejected Egyptian Slave." *Journal of Biblical Theology* 6, no. 2 (2023): 244.

Juster, Daniel C. "Ishmael and the Blessing of Abraham." In *Perspectives on Our Father Abraham: Essays in Honor of Marvin R. Wil-*

son, edited by Steven A. Hunt, 343–51. Grand Rapids: Eerdmans, 2010.

Longman, Tremper III, and David E. Garland, eds. *The Expositor's Bible Commentary: Genesis–Leviticus*. Revised Edition, vol. 1. Grand Rapids: Zondervan, 2008.

McKeown, James. *Genesis*. The Two Horizons Old Testament Commentary. Grand Rapids: Eerdmans, 2008.

Morris, Henry M. *The Genesis Record: A Scientific and Devotional Commentary on the Book of Beginnings*. Grand Rapids: Baker Book House, 1976. Kindle edition.

Ross, Allen P. *Genesis*. In *Cornerstone Biblical Commentary: Genesis and Exodus*, edited by Philip W. Comfort, vol. 1, 7–300. Carol Stream, IL: Tyndale House, 2008.

Sarna, Nahum M. *The JPS Torah Commentary: Genesis*. Philadelphia: Jewish Publication Society, 1989.

Schneider, Tammi J. *Mothers of Promise: Women in the Book of Genesis*. Grand Rapids: Baker Academic, 2008.

Shelley, A. Carter. *Preaching—Genesis 12–36*. St. Louis, MO: Chalice Press, 2001.

Towner, W. Sibley. *Genesis*. Westminster Bible Companion. Louisville: Westminster John Knox Press, 2001.

Trible, Phyllis. *Texts of Terror: Literary-Feminist Readings of Biblical Narratives*. 40th Anniversary Edition. Minneapolis: Fortress Press, 2022.

Trible, Phyllis, and Letty M. Russell, eds. *Hagar, Sarah, and Their Children: Jewish, Christian, and Muslim Perspectives*. Louisville, KY: Westminster John Knox Press, 2006.

Zucker, David J., and Moshe Reiss. *The Matriarchs of Genesis: Seven Women, Five Views*. Eugene, OR: Wipf & Stock, 2015. Kindle.

ABOUT THE AUTHOR

James S. Dorcely is a theologian, educator, and speaker who presents God not merely as the Author of our lives, but also as the Editor of our stories, reworking even the most painful chapters with redemptive love. He holds a Master of Divinity from Oral Roberts University and a Bachelor of Arts in Sociology from Montclair State University.

James serves in education and ministry leadership, where he teaches with compassion and builds bridges across diverse communities. His writing and teaching are shaped by what he calls The Whole Love Theology, a framework centered on restoring our relationship with God, with others, and with ourselves.

Through his books, articles, and teachings, James invites individuals to encounter a God who edits with purpose, compassion, and love.

For more information, visit his website at www.jamessdorcely.com or contact him via email at info@jamessdorcely.com.

www.ingramcontent.com/pod-product-compliance
Lightning Source LLC
Chambersburg PA
CBHW061354160726
47995CB00001B/310